THE STUDY OF POLITICS

T0345963

THE STUDY OF
POLITICS

BY

D. W. BROGAN

Professor of Political Science in the
University of Cambridge

AN INAUGURAL LECTURE
DELIVERED AT CAMBRIDGE ON
28 NOVEMBER 1945

CAMBRIDGE

At the University Press

1946

CAMBRIDGE
UNIVERSITY PRESS

University Printing House, Cambridge CB2 8BS, United Kingdom

Published in the United States of America by Cambridge University Press, New York

Cambridge University Press is part of the University of Cambridge.

It furthers the University's mission by disseminating knowledge in the pursuit of education, learning and research at the highest international levels of excellence.

www.cambridge.org
Information on this title: www.cambridge.org/9781107660366

© Cambridge University Press 1946

First published 1946
Re-issued 2014

A catalogue record for this publication is available from the British Library

ISBN 978-1-107-66036-6 Paperback

Cambridge University Press has no responsibility for the persistence or accuracy of URLs for external or third-party internet websites referred to in this publication, and does not guarantee that any content on such websites is, or will remain, accurate or appropriate.

THE
STUDY OF POLITICS

T HERE is something incongruous, possibly imperti-
nent, in offering to give an inaugural lecture more
than six years after this university had done me the
signal honour of electing me to succeed so great a scholar
as Sir Ernest Barker in the chair of Political Science. My
main, my only effectual excuse, must be the stress and
strain of war, the claims of other authorities than the university on what services I could perform. The alternative
was not the giving of an inaugural lecture earlier but the
not giving of it at all.

Yet that alternative, which has its attractions for human
idleness and timidity, was rejected by me and, I think,
rightly rejected. For there is a special duty incumbent on
a professor in a field like mine to declare the faith, or the
doubt, that is in him. He is not professing an exact science
in which his opinions, prejudices, views of his field of
study matter little. There may, indeed, be no such fields
of study, but if there are, the academic study of politics is
most certainly not one of them. To claim for it the
austerity and exactness, the freedom from the passions of
the hour that is the peculiar glory of those studies of which
this university is the most famous academic home, would
be absurd.

This seems to me to be a truth self-evident, but in
academic fashion, I fall back on the greatest name in the
long list of those who have written on politics in the

English tongue. It is true political science, true realism to assert with Burke that 'no reasonable man ever did govern himself by abstracts and universals'. Neither does nor did any society and the study of a field of human action in which passion and faith must play a great part must call, at any rate, surely may call for a modicum of passion and faith in the student?

If this be admitted, it is right that I should declare that I do not come to the study or teaching of politics a complete neutral, ready to believe that nothing has yet been decided or that all is eternally in question. I do not, so far, see my duties as those of a political seismologist content to note an earthquake here and a mere tremor there. Like Sir Ernest Barker, I think that the theme of politics is closely connected with ethics and especially 'with liberty as a part or element of the social aspect of goodness'. Such a confession will seem naïve to many, but to those who hold beliefs like mine it is some consolation to notice how hard it is for the adherents of more realist creeds, tied by first principles to more material concepts, to purge their vocabularies of the seductive words. And if those words are only used to seduce because of the resonance imparted to them by so many centuries of history, the mere habit of using them may not be without unforeseen results. For as Elie Halévy used to say, from the point of view of the statesman, of the public moralist, the homage of hypocrisy, paid by vice to virtue, is a real homage and may end in the conquest of the hypocrite by the virtues he has practised so long. To talk continually of liberty is dangerous, for the word may ask to be examined, and if examined may be found to have its old appeal. Be that as it may, the study of politics, as seen by me, is first of all and, perhaps, last of all, the study of the means whereby liberty and authority may be best combined, whereby the dignity of the free man is made compatible with the highest and richest forms of co-operation. For the art or science of politics, if it be more than a device for the acquisition of coercive power, must I think terminate in the creation or augmentation of men, not of things.

Had this chair been founded a century ago, the old Cambridge of mathematics tempered by classics might have been scandalized by the intrusion, but there would have been less scepticism as to the existence of a field of study called political science, although there might have been strong feeling that the proper place for such study was London or even Oxford. It may be surmised that there would have been fairly general agreement with the Society for the Diffusion of Useful Knowledge which began a lengthy work on *Political Philosophy* with a chapter entitled 'Advantages of Political Science'. True, in that chapter was admitted, handsomely, the superior precision of other disciplines.

'Mathematicians who run hardly any risk of error—naturalists who run but little more—have never been so bigoted and so uncharitable as those whose speculations are fated to be always involved more or less in doubt.' Having, from time to time, listened to the professional conversation of practitioners of these disciplines, I am a little inclined to see in this handsome testimonial an illustration of the well-known contrast between the reverence of the laity and the ironical levity of the priesthood. But the contrast with 'political reasoners' in whom 'we find beside the intolerance of metaphysicians, a new source of error and of fault in the excitement which the interests of men, real or supposed, lend to their passions', has still its old force. Indeed, it has more than its old force, for we may doubt to-day whether any such academic discipline as political science exists, a doubt practically unknown to earlier ages.

There is, it must be admitted, in the title of this chair, an ambiguity or a pretension that many find repellent. The direct connection of science with politics is infrequent, and that politics can be, in any but the most special sense, a science, may well be doubted. We can, of course, regard the whole of human experience as an unplanned biological experiment, providing data which, in their different ways, the historian, the economist, the sociologist, the political scientist studies and systematizes. And many, many books have been written on some such assumption. With few exceptions, however, the world has willingly let them die, and the rulers of the world have not been willing to go to school to such masters. So it was when Lemuel Gulliver happened to mention to the King of Brobdingnag that 'there were several thousand books among us written upon the *Art of Government*; it gave him (directly contrary to my intention) a very mean opinion of our Understandings'.

The King's opinion is widely shared and until a Darwin or Mendel comes among us to give a few general laws of political behaviour true of all species of political societies and of men in all their political relations, there is not much hope of changing this judgment of the world. In this sense 'political science' *is* a pretentious term, since its students and teachers do not acquire any such mastery of the political world as do physical scientists of the material world. Politics may have all the potentialities of the atomic bomb, but those potentialities are not the result of the activities of political scientists, as Plutonium or Neptunium are of the activities of the physicists.

When the whole problem of politics was the combination of liberty and effective authority and while there was still apparent agreement on the meaning, both of liberty and of effective and legitimate authority, the mechanisms of politics could be studied with the same optimistic attention as the mechanics which were transforming the industry and commerce of nations. Representative government was as happy and imitable an invention as the steam engine. Henry Hallam would have agreed with James Madison in admiration for the discovery of 'this great mechanical power in government, by the simple agency of which the will of the largest political body may be concentrated, and its force directed to any object which the public good requires'. This discovery relieved the optimistic political thinkers of the early nineteenth century from the fears of the incompatibility of power and freedom which had haunted Montesquieu and Rousseau. The fall of the Roman Empire was as much due to the failure of the Roman Republic to find this solution of its imperial problem, as to the incursion of the Barbarians, the influence of Christianity, or any accidents of history of the type of the length of Cleopatra's nose. The desperate remedy of Caesarism was made necessary by the failure to find the mild remedy of a representative Senate.

Dwelling in this climate of opinion, it was easy to delimit the field of political science, to put excessive faith (as even John Stuart Mill did) in mechanical devices like proportional representation, and see in the formal spread of representative government a ground for rejoicing and an invitation to study the ways in which the new Prussian or Japanese parliamentarism was imperfect though hopeful, the ways in which the congressional government of the United States diverged from a norm of which the House of Commons, or the total English system as described by Bagehot, was the exemplification.

The study of politics became, especially in the United States, a study of the mechanics of a society whose general character was taken for granted. Political mechanisms and ideas were added to a social structure; either they were forcibly imported and imposed as by the British in India, or were adopted by an awakening state as in Japan. If the adoption of western political principles and practices did not seem to give uniformly good results, or indeed uniform results of any kind, there were apparently adequate explanations to hand : race conflicts, illiteracy, backward religious beliefs and practices, debilitating climates, mere intellectual failure to grasp the rules of the game. So could the state of Mexico, of Italy, of Spain be accounted for. This type of explanation survived down into very recent times. It would be easy, but unkind, to exemplify it, to refer to a modern map illustrating the close correlation between illiteracy and dictatorial government, or to arguments assuming that once the Prussian military and civil bureaucracy was put under parliamentary control, the mere virtues of the parliamentary democratic system would work wonders, above all the wonder of replacing an old and deep-rooted German tradition with a new and foreign tradition. But to put it that way is to be unjust to the optimists who hardly considered the question of tradition at all, but saw the problem simply as the replacement of one mechanically conceived system of political organization by another.

We are, for the most part, cured of that illusion to-day. We have seen that universal literacy was no proof against the imposition of tyranny and that the most ingenious imitations of our political methods often, very often, failed to work. It has been seen that the question was not one of making minor modifications like the adjustment of a ship's piano to sail through the tropics, but of pondering the question, in no very optimistic frame of mind, 'Can any political mechanisms be usefully exported at all?' It was a useful reaction but it was too complete a reaction.

For the failures and the disillusionments of the old methods of comparative politics came from their too limited definition of the content of 'politics' and their failure to notice the relevance of other fields of comparative study. We have come to see the profound relevance of economic problems. We can see, for example, that the main Irish problem of the nineteenth century was the economic problem of the land system. We can see that the mere verbal imitation of the constitution of the United States of America by the United States of Mexico was bound to be a parody as long as the Mexican social structure was so different from the American, as long as there was no equivalent of the 'We the People of the United States', the concept and the political reality on which the constitution of the United States rested and rests.

It was and it is an easy reaction to dismiss the whole political apparatus as irrelevant and so its study as time-wasting pedantry. But such a view would be as far from realism as that of Broadbent in *John Bull's Other Island*. Broadbent, you will remember, could 'see no evils in the world—except, of course, natural evils—that cannot be remedied by freedom, self-government, and English institutions'. It was and is proper to laugh, but we can laugh too heartily and fail to notice that Broadbent was only exaggerating grossly, not talking mere nonsense. For freedom, self-government and English institutions have in practice cured or moderated very serious evils, from Suttee in India to child labour in England. The modern history of the Ireland in which Broadbent was pontificating would have been very different if there had not been English political institutions in England—and in Ireland. If you doubt that look at the very different history of Poland under the rule either of Prussia or of Russia. Because in Ireland the rulers and ruled talked the same political language, which both assumed was universally valid, they had a common ground on which to fight and argue and, on the stronger side, an increasing moral but none the less real compulsion to diminish the strain caused by the conflict between words and practice. Because there was a common political language and, if you will, a common superstition that political language mattered, the mere preponderance of power on one side was not given full weight. If you think that the matter of the dispute between England and Ireland was, once the basic land question was settled, of no real moment anyway, it is surely a very academic doctrine indeed that, in the name of realism, ignores what passions really move men to action!

And if the 'People of the United States' has become more and more a reality behind the text of the American constitution, it is because the constitution has proved, in practice, to be an effective environment for the real body politic to grow in.

When we laugh at the superstitious reverence of past generations for 'freedom, self-government and English institutions', we are in our right when we are laughing at an absurd and dangerous complacency, but we are not so much in our right when we laugh at the idea that freedom and self-government are or have been either good or important, or when we ignore the fact that they have been, in practice, associated with English institutions or colourable imitations of them. For the next stage is not to dismiss political institutions as unimportant, but to regard as virtues in other political institutions the mere absence of those qualities which Broadbent exalted with such complacency but not without good reason. Those qualities of a political system which Broadbent and an overwhelming majority of his countrymen prized for so long are, perhaps, not to be prized to-day. If this be so, I can only say with a Cambridge poet:

'Men are we and must grieve.'

I shall borrow, without permission but, I am certain, without objection from my predecessor, a justification of the university study of politics which Sir Ernest Barker applied to the general situation of democracy.

He listed among what he called the 'works of justification', the 'strengthening of the power of discussion—the broadening of civic intelligence and the extension of civic knowledge'. We must, in the university, do what is rightly declared to be the function and opportunity of the democratic state, 'enlist the effective thought of the whole community in the operation of discussion'.[1]

Here we are confronted with the difficulty that, whatever may be the case of the whole community of Britain, our university system, with its specialization and segregation, makes the 'enlistment of the whole community in the operation of discussion' difficult, perhaps impossible.

[1] Sir Ernest Barker, *Reflections on Government*, p. 414.

14

It is likely, indeed, that as far as we attain any enlistment of the university community 'in the operation of discussion' it will be by reflecting back from the national community such degree of candour and unity as the nation may have attained. There is nothing, alas, in the history of universities, even of this university, that suggests any immunity from passion inherent in the institution or in its teachers and students. But that weakness has arisen, in part at least, from the tacit acceptance of the view that politics was not a fit subject for university discussion or for the application of university standards or methods.

In such a frame of mind it was easy to admire the attitude of the Warden of Judas in the other place, 'year following year in ornamental seclusion from the follies and fusses of the world'. But the world has a way of forcing its follies and fusses on us, even on the two ancient universities. And in the home of the Cavendish laboratory, it is not irrelevant to point out that the universities have their way of intruding, decisively, on the fusses and follies of the world.

At this moment in world history, when the contrast between man's command over nature, almost over the processes of creation, and his power of command over his own society has never been so great or so terrifying, it is unnecessary to stress the importance of politics. It is politics that fills the world with fear; it is political failure that is the greatest menace to 'life, liberty and the pursuit of happiness'. In bad politics is our doom; in good politics is our only hope of salvation.

What can a university do to encourage what I have called good politics? It cannot and it should not attempt to train statesmen; they are artists, no more to be produced by universities than are great painters by the multiplication of art schools. Yet great artists have come out of art schools none the worse for it, and great statesmen have come out of universities possibly even the better for it. Nor is the idea of making a university education part of the foundation on which the future politician and ruler builds, really novel. To go no further back than the last great century, it was an admitted function of the mathematical tripos in this university, of the school of *Literae Humaniores* in Oxford, to give to the future member of Parliament, cabinet minister, ruler of India, a view of the world of state that would, it was hoped, raise them above the mere 'bustle of local agency' deprecated by Burke. It may be objected that any good university education will do that, and that the more exact and traditional academic studies do it better than those too much mingled with the business of the day. The first thesis I should not, for a moment, deny; the second I am, in a sense, debarred from accepting as long as I draw the stipend of this chair. But even did I hold the older academic view, I should feel myself bound to notice that the world expects the universities to have wider interests than the teaching of the young; they exist for the advancement of learning as well as its transmission. And we must also notice that the taught have their choices and if denied the gratification of them, if forced to accept the old fortifying curriculum, will not thereby be prevented from seeking the food they crave elsewhere. It is then too late to rebuke the young for being

'swoln with wind, and the rank mist they draw'

or even, to amend Milton, reproach them that they

'rot outwardly and foul contagion spread'.

It is now too late to save the university 'from the contagion of the world's slow stain'; it always has been. And it is to be noted that Shelley wrote this after being sent down for extra-curricular politics.

If the university is to teach politics, it is sufficient justification and sufficient guide to its methods of teaching that the job is in any case being done by others, outside the university, and so it had better be done inside it. I have already suggested that it is vain to expect of the teaching or teachers of politics that they should be as exact or neutral as the traditional teacher of mathematics or grammar. We must not try to impose on the teaching of politics a degree of abstractness or bogus neutrality which it cannot stand. But we *can* bring to its study auxiliaries that are not so easily called on by the outside world. First of all we must bring the aid of history. This university has wisely provided for the case of any professor holding this chair who might be tempted to deny this, by attaching him to the History Board in the first place as well as to the Board of Economics and Politics. But even were there not this legal bond, there is the bond imposed by the nature of the study. 'History is past politics', said a Cambridge professor. He was only very partially right, but present politics is always at least half history. It is natural and, indeed, right that we should regret this, for the history that is present politics is mainly composed of envy, malice and all uncharitableness. But we must understand the world before we can hope to change it and that is our world. It is useless merely to rail against it. We must use good history, scholarly history, to drive out bad; we may be sure that there are all the devils possible already in possession and that the broom of historical scholarship will do something to make the house of nations more habitable.

Then we must bring to our students' minds—and perpetually recall to our own—those great minds of the past who have pondered the perennial problems of man in society and in the state. Their relevance is not that they give us blue prints, but that they make us see, and feel, and think in a fashion that our unaided faculties would not enable us to do. The young are more likely to appreciate the dictum of a late master of Trinity that denies infallibility even to youth, when that lesson is taught them by Plato or Burke, than when it is taught them by a living and palpably misguided mortal like a professor.

The mind of a great thinker of the past may suddenly illuminate the mind, not only of the average man, but of the very exceptional man as, on their own testimony, the *Republic* did for Mr Shaw and Mr Wells. And when these great minds of the past are illuminated by a great scholar in the present, as Plato and Aristotle were by my predecessor, there is hardly any need to justify the teaching of politics in this exalted and elevating sense.

But there are other academic aids to breeding in the young more understanding of the world they very reasonably want to change. Although it was necessity, not any prevision of self-improvement, that led to the postponement to 1945 of an inaugural lecture that should have been delivered in 1939, that delay has been, for me at any rate, of great value. I held then the general views I hold now, but my views as to the scope and method of the study of politics have been altered and, I naturally think, improved. I am by equipment, by temperament and by limitations a student of political institutions. I am incapable of changing, of becoming a political philosopher or a philosophical historian. But I have learned in the past six years, by non-academic work, by reflection and by reading, even by writing, that the student of political institutions must be much more than that. He must be purged of the idea that political institutions exist in a vacuum or that they can be understood apart from other institutions. That, as I have suggested, was the great error of the public-spirited, highly intelligent, and highly effective makers of the modern liberal tradition. Politics could not be separated from many non-political habits and institutions. New political institutions could at best be grafted, they could not merely be soldered on.

The realization of this truth would not be helpful or encouraging if we had no more means of studying these related social institutions than we had a hundred years ago,

in the prematurely confident days of Bentham, Comte,
Marx and other founders of great and influential schools
of political and social doctrine. But we are, in fact, much
better equipped to understand society and mankind than
our great predecessors were. It is only necessary to turn
to the anthropology, the psychology, the sociology of a
century ago to see how much that seems commonplace to
us was then unknown. For good or ill, Freud and Frazer,
Marx and Darwin, Maine and Maitland have passed by.
The organization of primitive society is far better known;
the survival in our society of primitive elements is far
better realized. We shrink from the simply rational explanation; we shrink too much I feel, but we have learned
that we see (all philosophical scepticism apart) very darkly
indeed through the imperfect glass left us by our ancestors.
The full enlightenment, we know to-day, is still far ahead
of us; it may be permanently ahead of us.

But this 'scepticism of the instrument', to borrow a
phrase from Mr Wells, should not and need not reduce us
to a resigned acceptance of our inheritance. We can, if we
like, fall back on what American sociologists call the
'mores' or, more pedantically, the 'folkways' and, in a
new and debased form of determinism, assume readily
that we cannot alter them, we can only accept them,
describe them, classify and explain them. So Indian
sociologists a century ago (had they existed then) might
have passively regarded Suttee or Thuggee. So did not
Lord William Bentinck or his energetic 'brains trust',
young Mr Macaulay late of Trinity.

There is no need for passivity or pessimism and it is my suspicion that the passivity or pessimism, in most exponents of the doctrine of the practical impossibility even of gradualness, has more temperamental than strictly intellectual roots. But the study of society and of man, of the institutions, the traditions, the historical conditions that limit and impose direction on purely political activity, is certainly far more possible to-day than it has ever been in human history. And a university school of politics, should one come into existence, would be bound to take a far wider view of the content of its teaching and researches than a mere professor of Political Science can afford to do. All that he can do is to avert his eyes from the lavish provision for such related studies in the great American universities, and return to his own narrower field.

Politics in the university sense can be taught, can be researched on. The politician in the university sense has the duty, in his teaching and writing, in his encouragement of the teaching and writing of others, to import into this double activity as much of the standards of university teaching and research as the mixed and troublesome nature of his subject will permit. As the politician himself is the specialist in not being a specialist, the academic politician must suffer the qualms that beset the practitioner of a slightly suspect mystery. He must not worry if he is called a bone-setter, *if* he can be sure that he has at least once set even quite a small bone. He may be well advised to stay out of politics, national or university, and I gather from the late Professor Cornford that the rigours of the game are as great in King's Parade or the Senate House as in Westminster or Tammany Hall.

But his main duty will be to teach and exemplify a view of politics once advanced by a then obscure, practising politician in face of a great national crisis. 'If we could first know where we are, and whither we are tending, we could better judge what to do, and how to do it.' What Abraham Lincoln said, in his first great speech, seems banal enough. But platitudinous as it is, it is a platitude to be repeated and insinuated into the public mind in every generation and in every crisis. If, as Chesterton said, 'the world will never be made safe for democracy, it is a dangerous trade', the main reason is that the platitudes of politics are forever being forgotten, the forts of folly being rebuilt with formidable speed. The university contribution to politics must often take the dull form of reiterating old truth; it can also take the form of developing new and deeper understanding of those truths and, lastly, it can take the form of teaching, by example, that it matters a great deal with what cannon and what ammunition you assail the forts of folly. The example of the other studies of this university and of all other true *studia generalia* may, and I hope will, teach this terribly threatened generation that more permanent victories are won by clearer heads and cleaner hands than the world, left to itself, will suggest to the practising politician that he should use.